JOHN WOLFF

Get Answers to Your Tax Questions

Your Essential Guide to Individual Federal Taxes

Copyright © 2024 by John Wolff

All rights reserved. No part of this publication may be reproduced, stored or transmitted in any form or by any means, electronic, mechanical, photocopying, recording, scanning, or otherwise without written permission from the publisher. It is illegal to copy this book, post it to a website, or distribute it by any other means without permission.

John Wolff has no responsibility for the persistence or accuracy of URLs for external or third-party Internet Websites referred to in this publication and does not guarantee that any content on such Websites is, or will remain, accurate or appropriate.

Designations used by companies to distinguish their products are often claimed as trademarks. All brand names and product names used in this book and on its cover are trade names, service marks, trademarks and registered trademarks of their respective owners. The publishers and the book are not associated with any product or vendor mentioned in this book. None of the companies referenced within the book have endorsed the book.

First edition

This book was professionally typeset on Reedsy.
Find out more at reedsy.com

Contents

Introduction	1
Chapter 1 - The Basic of Taxes	3
Question 1: What Are Taxes and Why Do We Pay Them?	3
Question 2: How Do Taxes Work?	4
Chapter 2 - Starting Off	6
Question 3: When Do I Need to Start Filing Taxes?	6
Question 4: What's the Difference Between Being Employed and Self-Employed for Tax Purposes?	7
Chapter 3 - Filing Your Taxes	9
Question 5: What Documents Do I Need to File My Taxes?	9
Question 6: How Do I Choose the Right Form to File My Taxes?	10
Question 7: Can I File My Taxes Online, and How?	11
Chapter 4 - Common Deductions and Credits	13
Question 8: What Are Tax Deductions and Credits?	13
Question 9: Can I Deduct My College Tuition?	14
Question 10: Are There Deductions for Freelancers or Side Gigs?	14
Chapter 5 - Handling Tax Problems	16
Question 11: What If I Make a Mistake on My Tax Return?	16
Question 12: What Happens If I Can't Pay My Taxes on Time?	17

Question 13: How Do I Know If I Need to Amend a Previous Tax Return?	17
Chapter 6 - Planning for the Future	19
Question 14: How Can Taxes Affect My Savings and Investment Choices?	19
Question 15: What Tax Advantages Do Retirement Accounts Offer?	20
Question 16: How Do Marriage and Children Impact My Taxes?	21
Chapter 7 - Advanced Tax Questions	22
Question 17: What Is an Audit, and Why Does It Happen?	22
Question 18: How Can I Prepare for the Possibility of an Audit?	23
Question 19: What Are Estimated Taxes, and Who Needs to Pay Them?	23
Chapter 8 – Additional Tax Tips	25
Question 20: How Do I Keep Track of My Expenses and Deductions Throughout the Year?	25
Question 21: What Are Some Common Tax Mistakes to Avoid?	26
Question 22: When Should I Consult with a Tax Accountant?	27
Chapter 9 - The Future of Taxes	28
Question 23: How Might Tax Laws Change in the Future, and How Can I Stay Informed?	28
Question 24: What Are Digital Currencies, and How Are They Taxed?	29
Question 25: Are There New Tax Credits or Deductions I Should Be Aware Of?	30
Conclusion	31
Glossary: Understanding Key Tax Terms	34
Useful Tools and Links for Managing Taxes	37

Resources 40

Introduction

Welcome to your financial toolkit! This book is designed to help you learn about personal individual taxes. The purpose of this book is to encourage you to explore the tax basics by addressing questions you might be hesitant to ask. Think of it as a bridge over the vast sea of financial knowledge, providing a safe and clear path by tackling common tax concerns, clearing up misconceptions, and breaking down complex concepts into easy-to-understand information.

This book creates an environment where every question is simple and realistic. Whether you are curious about how taxes work, looking for the best ways to save on taxes legally, or wondering when it is the right time to hire a tax accountant, this guide has you covered. Using a question-and-answer format mirrors the natural curiosity that fuels learning and growth, reassuring you that asking questions is not just part of learning—it is the heart of it.

Moreover, this book aims to spark everyone's interest in personal finance management. It is about being proactive with taxes and accounting, not just as a necessity but as an opportunity. An opportunity to take control of your financial future, maximize savings, and make informed decisions that align with your personal and professional goals.

Essentially, this guide is more than just a book about taxes and accounting; it is a toolkit for financial empowerment. By simplifying the complex world of financial terminology and regulations, we aim to transform apprehension into action, fear into understanding, and confusion into clarity. Encouraging you to ask questions is the first step in this transformative journey, leading you toward a more informed, confident, and financially savvy future. Let's dive in!

Chapter 1 - The Basic of Taxes

Welcome to the world of taxes! If you've ever wondered why a portion of your paycheck disappears before you even see it or why people often talk about tax time with a mix of dread and acceptance, you're in the right place. This chapter will explain taxes, why they're a part of our lives, and how they work in simple terms. Let's begin!

Question 1: What Are Taxes and Why Do We Pay Them?

Imagine playing a multiplayer online game where everyone contributes some of their in-game currency to keep the game running smoothly. This contribution helps maintain the game servers, develop new content, and ensure that everyone has a good gaming experience. In real life, taxes are similar. They are contributions that we all make to the big "game" called society.

Taxes are payments made to the government by individuals and businesses. But unlike paying for a product or service, where you directly see what you're getting, taxes fund the collective needs and services of the entire community. This includes schools, roads, hospitals, police and fire services, and much more. In essence, paying taxes is how we pool our resources to make sure our communities have the essentials we all rely on.

Why do we pay them? Because these services, from education to infrastructure to national defense, are critical for the country's functioning and the well-being of its citizens. Taxes ensure that these services can be provided without direct charges every time they are used.

Question 2: How Do Taxes Work?

Understanding how taxes work can seem like learning a new language. Let's simplify it:

1. **Tax Brackets**: Think of tax brackets as levels in a game. The more money you make, the higher your level, and different rules (tax rates) apply. The United States uses a progressive tax system, meaning the more income you earn, the higher the tax rate you'll pay on your top dollar. However, due to these brackets, only some of your income is taxed at the same rate, which helps keep the system fairer.
2. **Deductions:** Deductions are like special power-ups that reduce how much of your income can be taxed. Common deductions include money spent on certain business expenses, education, and donations to charity. By lowering your taxable income, these deductions can decrease the amount of tax you owe.
3. **Credits:** Tax credits are even more powerful than deductions. They are dollar-for-dollar reductions in the amount of tax you owe. Think of them as coupons that can reduce your tax bill directly rather than just reducing the amount of income that gets taxed. Some credits support going to college, investing in renewable energy, or having children.

In a nutshell, taxes are a way for everyone to contribute to the common good, ensuring that our society has the resources it needs to function.

CHAPTER 1 - THE BASIC OF TAXES

Through a system of brackets, deductions, and credits, the tax system aims to be fair, rewarding certain behaviors (like saving for retirement or going to college) while ensuring that the more you earn, the more you contribute. Understanding these basics can help clarify your tax bill and show you how your contributions are essential to the bigger picture.

Chapter 2 - Starting Off

Navigating the world of taxes can feel like setting off on an epic journey without a map. But don't worry; we're here to guide you through the early stages of this adventure. This chapter will help you understand when to start filing taxes and explain the differences between being employed and self-employed for tax purposes.

Question 3: When Do I Need to Start Filing Taxes?

You might think that you only need to start worrying about taxes once you've landed your first full-time job. However, the truth is a bit more nuanced. The need to file a tax return depends on several factors, including your age, income level, and specific circumstances. Here's a simplified breakdown:

1. **Income Levels:** The IRS sets income thresholds that determine who needs to file a tax return. These thresholds can change yearly and depend on your filing status (such as single, married filing jointly, etc.). Generally, if you earn more than the standard deduction for your filing status, you'll need to file a tax return. For young adults and teenagers, even part-time jobs or freelance gigs can mean you have to file if you earn above a certain amount.
2. **Dependent Status:** If you're still considered a dependent on

someone else's tax return (like a parent's), different rules apply. Dependents have lower income thresholds for filing taxes, meaning you might need to file a return even if you make less money than independent adults.
3. **Self-Employment:** If you're self-employed and make $400 or more in a year, you must file a tax return. This rule catches many young entrepreneurs and freelancers by surprise, so it's crucial to keep track of your earnings if you're making money through a side hustle or your own business.

Question 4: What's the Difference Between Being Employed and Self-Employed for Tax Purposes?

The distinction between being employed and self-employed significantly impacts how you handle your taxes. Here's what you need to know:

1. **Employed:** If you work for an employer (you receive a W-2 form), your employer will withhold taxes from your paycheck. This includes federal and state income taxes, Social Security, and Medicare taxes. Your employer calculates your withholding based on the information you provide in your W-4 form when you start your job. At the end of the year, filing your tax return reconciles what you've already paid against what you owe. If too much was withheld, you might get a refund; if too little was withheld, you might owe more.
2. **Self-Employed:** Being self-employed (you receive a 1099 form) means you are responsible for paying your taxes directly to the IRS and state tax authorities. These taxes include not only income taxes but also self-employment taxes, which cover your Social Security and Medicare contributions. Since there's no employer

to withhold taxes from your paychecks, you may need to make estimated tax payments throughout the year to avoid a large tax bill and potential penalties when you file your return.

The critical difference lies in who manages the tax withholdings and payments. Employed individuals have some of this process handled by their employers, while self-employed individuals are entirely responsible for managing their tax obligations.

Understanding these basics can help you navigate your tax journey's early decisions and responsibilities. Whether you are earning your first paycheck from a part-time job or launching your freelance career, knowing when to file and the implications of your employment status are crucial first steps.

Chapter 3 - Filing Your Taxes

Filing taxes might seem like a daunting task, especially if it's your first time. But fear not! You can confidently tackle tax filing with the right documents and a basic understanding of the process. Let's break down the essentials: the documents you need, choosing the correct tax form, and the steps to file your taxes online.

Question 5: What Documents Do I Need to File My Taxes?

Before you start, gathering all necessary documents is crucial. This checklist will help ensure you have everything you need:

Personal Information:

- Social Security Number (SSN) or Individual Taxpayer Identification Number (ITIN) for yourself, your spouse, and dependents (if any).
- Bank account and routing numbers for direct deposit of your refund.

Income Documents:

- W-2 forms from all employers you worked for during the year.
- 1099-NEC or 1099-MISC forms if you're self-employed.

- 1099-INT if you have earned interest.
- 1099-DIV if you have received dividends.
- Documents for other sources of income (rental income, savings, investments, etc.)

Deduction Documents:

- Receipts for charitable donations
- Medical and dental expenses
- Education expenses (Form 1098-T for tuition)
- Mortgage interest statements (Form 1098).

Tax Credits Information:

- Documents supporting eligibility for credits include childcare expenses, education costs, and retirement savings contributions.

Previous Year's Tax Return: Helpful as a reference and often required if you're using a new tax filing service or accountant.

Question 6: How Do I Choose the Right Form to File My Taxes?

The IRS provides different forms depending on your specific tax situation:

- **Form 1040:** The standard form for individual tax filers, encompassing various income types, deductions, and credits. Most taxpayers will use this form.
- **Form 1040-SR:** Designed for senior citizens, offering a larger print and a focus on retirement income but essentially similar to Form

1040.
- **Form 1040-NR:** For non-resident aliens engaging in business in the U.S. or receiving U.S. income.

Your choice among these depends on your residency status, age, and types of income. The IRS' website offers a "Which Form Should I Use?" tool that provides guidance based on personal information.

Question 7: Can I File My Taxes Online, and How?

Yes, filing taxes online is not only possible but recommended for its ease and quicker processing times. Here's how to do it:

1. **Choose a Filing Service**: Many IRS-approved e-file providers exist, including TurboTax, H&R Block, and the IRS's own Free File for those who qualify based on income. Compare services to find one that matches your needs and budget.
2. **Gather Your Documents:** Use the checklist above for all necessary information.
3. **Create an Account:** If it's your first time using the service, you'll need to create an account. Returning users can log in to access past information, saving time.
4. **Follow the Steps:** The online service will guide you through entering your information, from personal details to income, deductions, and credits. It automatically selects the correct form for you.
5. **Review and Submit:** Before submitting, review your return for any errors. Once satisfied, file your taxes electronically. You'll receive a confirmation email from the IRS once they accept your return.
6. **Track Your Refund:** If you expect a refund, you can track its

GET ANSWERS TO YOUR TAX QUESTIONS

status through the IRS's "Where's My Refund?" tool.

- If you file electronically and have the refund deposited directly into your bank account, it usually takes about 21 days. If you file a tax return on paper, it can take up to 2 months or longer.
- To use the IRS Tool, you will need your Social Security number, filing status, and the exact dollar amount of your expected refund.

By following these steps, you can tackle tax filing with confidence. Remember, the key to a smooth tax filing experience is preparation. With the proper documents in hand, understanding which form fits your situation, and the convenience of online filing, you're well-equipped to manage your taxes efficiently.

Chapter 4 - Common Deductions and Credits

Understanding tax deductions and credits can significantly reduce your tax bill, making them crucial elements of tax filing. Though they might sound similar, they work quite differently in practice. Let's explore these terms and how you can qualify for them. We will also dive into specific examples related to education expenses and deductions for freelancers or those with side gigs.

Question 8: What Are Tax Deductions and Credits?

Tax deductions lower your taxable income. Think of them as discounts on the amount of your income that is subject to tax. For example, if you earn $50,000 and have $5,000 in deductions, you'll only be taxed on $45,000. Common deductions include charitable donations, mortgage interest, and certain business expenses.

Tax credits, on the other hand, are like gift cards applied directly to your tax bill. If you owe $1,000 in taxes and are eligible for a $200 tax credit, you only need to pay $800. Credits can be refundable or non-refundable. Refundable credits can get you a refund even if you don't owe any taxes, while non-refundable credits can only lower your bill to $0.

GET ANSWERS TO YOUR TAX QUESTIONS

Question 9: Can I Deduct My College Tuition?

Yes, education expenses, including college tuition, can qualify for deductions and credits, making them a significant opportunity for students and their families.

- **The American Opportunity Tax Credit (AOTC)** offers up to $2,500 per eligible student for the first four years of higher education. This credit covers expenses like tuition, course materials, and required fees. If the credit brings your tax liability to zero, 40% of the remaining amount (up to $1,000) can be refunded.
- **The Lifetime Learning Credit (LLC)** provides up to $2,000 per tax return (not per student) and applies to tuition and fees for undergraduate, graduate, and professional degree courses, including courses to acquire or improve job skills. Unlike the AOTC, it's not limited to the first four years of post-secondary education; there's no limit on the number of years you can claim it.
- **Tuition and Fees Deduction** was available to reduce taxable income; however, this deduction has been phased out in favor of the credits mentioned above.

Question 10: Are There Deductions for Freelancers or Side Gigs?

Freelancers and individuals with side gigs have a unique tax situation but also benefit from numerous deductions to lower their taxable income. Here are some deductions to consider:

- **Home Office Deduction:** If you use part of your home exclusively for business, you may deduct expenses related to that portion, such

CHAPTER 4 - COMMON DEDUCTIONS AND CREDITS

as a percentage of rent or mortgage interest, utilities, and insurance.

- **Supplies and Equipment:** Purchases necessary for your business, like computers, software, and office supplies, are deductible.
- **Travel and Mileage:** You can deduct the costs associated with business travel, including mileage, airfare, and lodging.
- **Education and Training:** Courses or workshops to improve your business skills or expertise are deductible.
- **Health Insurance Premiums:** Self-employed individuals can deduct medical, dental, and qualifying long-term care insurance premiums for themselves and their dependents.

As a reminder, business expenses should be ordinary and necessary for your specific business. Understanding the distinctions between deductions and credits and knowing what you're eligible for can significantly impact your tax situation. Whether you're navigating education expenses or managing income from freelance work or side gigs, there are many opportunities to reduce your tax liability and increase your refund. Always keep accurate records and consider consulting a tax professional to maximize these benefits.

Chapter 5 - Handling Tax Problems

Even the most careful of us can run into tax problems, whether it's a mistake on a return or difficulty paying on time. The good news is there's always a way to address these issues. Let's explore how to handle some common tax problems so you can resolve them without too much stress.

Question 11: What If I Make a Mistake on My Tax Return?

Firstly, don't panic. If you discover an error on your tax return, the IRS usually gives taxpayers the chance to correct mistakes without severe penalties, especially if they're honest errors. Here's what you can do:

- **Small Errors:** The IRS often corrects minor mistakes like math errors during processing and will notify you of any changes. In these cases, you may not need to do anything.
- **Significant Errors:** If the mistake affects your income, deductions, or credits, you must file an amended tax return using Form 1040-X. This form allows you to correct previously filed information and explain the changes.

CHAPTER 5 - HANDLING TAX PROBLEMS

Question 12: What Happens If I Can't Pay My Taxes on Time?

Facing a tax bill from the IRS that you cannot pay is stressful, but ignoring it is the worst strategy. Here's what to do instead:

- **File on Time:** Always file your return on time, even if you can't pay the total amount. By filing your return, you avoid a late filing penalty, which can add more to your bill.
- **Contact the IRS:** The IRS offers payment plans for individuals who can't pay their taxes in full. You can apply for a short-term extension to pay, a long-term payment plan, or even an offer in compromise, which might settle your tax debt for less than the total amount owed.
- **Consider Your Options:** Consider using a credit card or loan to pay your tax bill. Sometimes, the interest on these might be lower than the combined penalties and interest the IRS charges for late payments.

Question 13: How Do I Know If I Need to Amend a Previous Tax Return?

Consider amending a return if you need to correct your filing status, income, deductions, or credits. Here's how to decide if you need to file an amended return:

- **Review Changes Carefully:** If you forgot to include income, didn't claim a credit you were eligible for, or made a significant mistake on your return, amending is likely necessary.
- **Timing:** You can file an amended return up to three years after filing your original tax return or two years after paying the tax,

whichever is later.
- **Filing an Amended Return:** Use Form 1040-X to amend your return. You can file amended returns electronically for certain tax years, but you may need to mail in a paper copy for others. Always check the latest IRS guidelines.

Handling tax problems responsibly and proactively can mitigate the impact on your finances and stress levels. Whether correcting an error, dealing with a payment issue, or amending a past return, the key is to act quickly and utilize your resources and options. Remember, the IRS is more accommodating to those who make a genuine effort to resolve their tax issues.

Chapter 6 - Planning for the Future

When you think about your financial future, taxes might not be the first thing that comes to mind. However, understanding how taxes can impact your savings, investments, and family planning is crucial for long-term financial health. This chapter will explore tax-efficient strategies for saving and investing, the benefits of retirement accounts, and the implications of marriage and children on your taxes.

Question 14: How Can Taxes Affect My Savings and Investment Choices?

Taxes can significantly impact the return on your investments and savings. By making tax-efficient choices, you can maximize your after-tax returns, keeping more money in your pocket. Here are some tips:

- **Consider Tax-Advantaged Accounts:** Investing in accounts like Roth IRAs or 529 college savings plans can offer tax-free growth or withdrawals, making them excellent options for long-term savings.
- **Understand Capital Gains Taxes:** Investments held for over a year qualify for long-term capital gains rates, which are generally lower than short-term rates for assets held for less than a year. Planning your sales around these rules can save you on taxes.
- **Use Tax-Loss Harvesting:** This strategy involves selling invest-

ments at a loss to offset gains in other areas of your portfolio, potentially reducing your taxable income.

Question 15: What Tax Advantages Do Retirement Accounts Offer?

Retirement accounts like IRAs and 401(k)s are not just savings tools but also powerful tax planning instruments. Here's how they can benefit you:

- **Traditional IRAs and 401(k)s:** Contributions to these accounts may be tax-deductible, reducing your taxable income in the contribution year. Taxes on earnings are deferred until withdrawals begin, typically in retirement when you may be in a lower tax bracket.
- **Roth IRAs and Roth 401(k)s:** Contributions are made with after-tax dollars, but withdrawals in retirement are tax-free, including the earnings. This can be a significant advantage if you expect to be in a higher tax bracket in the future.
- **Contribution Limits and Tax Deductions:** Both account types have annual contribution limits and rules about deductions, so staying informed about current regulations is essential to maximize these benefits.

CHAPTER 6 - PLANNING FOR THE FUTURE

Question 16: How Do Marriage and Children Impact My Taxes?

Changes in your family structure can significantly affect your taxes, often in beneficial ways:

- **Marriage:** Couples have the option to file taxes jointly or separately. Joint filing usually offers more tax benefits, such as higher income thresholds for tax brackets and deductions. However, it's crucial to calculate taxes both ways to determine which filing status is more advantageous for your situation.
- **Children:** Having children can qualify you for various tax credits and deductions, including the Child Tax Credit, Child and Dependent Care Credit, and the Earned Income Tax Credit. These benefits can significantly reduce your tax liability.
- **Filing Status and Exemptions:** Your filing status, such as head of household, can also impact your tax rates and standard deductions. Understanding how to leverage your family status can lead to substantial tax savings.

By incorporating tax planning into your long-term financial strategy, you can take advantage of various savings and investment opportunities to maximize your wealth over time. Whether choosing the right retirement accounts, understanding the benefits of marriage and children on your taxes, or employing tax-efficient investment strategies, a little knowledge can go a long way in securing your financial future.

Chapter 7 - Advanced Tax Questions

As you become more familiar with the basics of taxes, it's time to tackle some advanced topics that can seem intimidating at first glance. Understanding audits, preparing for them, and navigating estimated taxes are crucial for anyone, especially if you're self-employed or running a business. Let's clarify these aspects.

Question 17: What Is an Audit, and Why Does It Happen?

An audit is the IRS' way of double-checking your numbers to ensure you've paid the correct amount of taxes. While the thought of an audit can be scary, most are straightforward: you provide additional information to the IRS, and they confirm your tax return is accurate.

Audits can happen for several reasons, some of which might include:

- **Random Selection:** Sometimes, returns are chosen randomly for an audit.
- **Discrepancies:** Mismatches between what you report and information the IRS receives (e.g., W-2s, 1099s) can trigger an audit.
- **Excessive Deductions:** Claiming significantly higher deductions or credits than the norm for your income level can raise red flags.
- **Charity:** If you contribute $250 or more to a charity, you will

need a letter documenting the gift. If more than $5,000, additional record-keeping requirements, such as an appraisal on the item.

Question 18: How Can I Prepare for the Possibility of an Audit?

While you can't always prevent an audit, you can prepare for the possibility. Here are some tips:

- **Keep Good Records:** Maintain detailed records of income, deductions, and credits. Receipts, bank statements, and logs are essential.
- **Understand Your Return:** Know why you're eligible for the deductions and credits you claim. If you use a tax preparer, ask questions to understand your return fully.
- **Stay Organized:** Keep tax documents for at least three years from the date you filed your original return, as this is generally the period the IRS can initiate an audit. Or six years if you have self-employed income. It's a good rule of thumb to keep your tax returns forever to be on the safe side.

Question 19: What Are Estimated Taxes, and Who Needs to Pay Them?

Estimated taxes are periodic payments made to the IRS by people who earn income and are not subject to withholding taxes. This typically includes freelancers, entrepreneurs, and some investors. You'll likely need to make estimated tax payments if you owe $1,000 or more when your return is filed.

Estimated taxes are paid quarterly, and the amounts are based on your expected adjusted gross income, taxable income, taxes, deductions, and credits for the year. Here's how to manage them:

- **Calculate Your Estimated Tax**: Use Form 1040-ES to estimate your taxes for the year. This form includes a worksheet that helps you estimate your income and the taxes you owe.
- **Make Payments Quarterly:** The IRS has set deadlines for estimated tax payments, typically April 15, June 15, September 15, and January 15 (of the following year).
- **Adjust as Needed:** If your income changes significantly during the year, adjust your estimated payments accordingly to avoid underpaying or overpaying.

Understanding and managing estimated taxes are crucial for freelancers and entrepreneurs to avoid surprises come tax time. By keeping detailed financial records and planning quarterly payments, you can ensure you're meeting your tax obligations without stress.

Navigating advanced tax questions like audits and estimated taxes might seem daunting, but with the right knowledge and preparation, you can handle these aspects of your taxes confidently. Whether it is keeping meticulous records to prepare for a potential audit or accurately calculating estimated taxes, being proactive about your tax responsibilities can save you time and trouble in the long run.

Chapter 8 – Additional Tax Tips

Diving deeper into the realm of taxes, it's crucial to build good habits around financial organization, be aware of common pitfalls, and understand when it's wise to seek professional advice. This chapter will equip you with strategies to manage your expenses and deductions effectively, highlight common tax mistakes to avoid, and guide you on consulting with a tax accountant.

Question 20: How Do I Keep Track of My Expenses and Deductions Throughout the Year?

Keeping a meticulous record of your expenses and potential deductions can make tax time significantly less stressful. It can ensure you don't miss out on any opportunities to reduce your tax bill. Here are some strategies to stay organized:

- **Use Financial Tracking Apps:** Many apps are designed to track your spending and categorize expenses, some even specifically for tax deductions. This digital approach can simplify the process of sorting through your financial records at the end of the year.
- **Maintain a Dedicated File System:** Whether you prefer digital or paper files, create a system for organizing receipts, invoices, and documents relevant to your taxes. Consider monthly folders or

categories based on the type of expense or income.
- **Regularly Update Records:** Set aside time monthly or quarterly to update your records. This habit prevents the overwhelming task of sorting through a year's worth of documents at once.

Question 21: What Are Some Common Tax Mistakes to Avoid?

Even with the best intentions, stumbling into common tax pitfalls is easy. Awareness is the first step toward avoidance:

- **Not Filing Taxes Because of Low Income**: Many young adults miss out on potential refunds by assuming they don't need to file taxes due to their low income. Even if your income is below the filing threshold, you may be eligible for refundable tax credits.
- **Ignoring Tax Documents:** Failing to report all income, including from part-time jobs or freelance work, can lead to IRS penalties. Make sure to keep and use all your received tax documents when filing.
- **Forgetting About Deductions and Credits:** Overlooking education credits, deductions for student loan interest, or charitable donations can mean paying more tax than necessary. Educate yourself on what deductions and credits you might be eligible for.

CHAPTER 8 – ADDITIONAL TAX TIPS

Question 22: When Should I Consult with a Tax Accountant?

While not everyone needs to see a tax accountant annually, certain situations make consulting one beneficial:

- **Significant Life Changes:** Marriage, buying a house, or starting a business can all complicate your tax situation. A professional can help you navigate these changes.
- **Self-Employment:** Freelancers and entrepreneurs face complex tax obligations, from estimated tax payments to business deductions. Regular consultations can ensure you're on track and taking advantage of all available tax benefits.
- **Investment Income:** If you have income from investments, rental properties, or other sources beyond a traditional salary, an accountant or financial adviser can help optimize your tax strategy.

As a rule of thumb, even if you don't think you need to see a tax accountant every year, scheduling a consultation every few years can ensure you're not missing out on tax-saving opportunities. Keeping organized records and being aware of common mistakes can help make these consultations more effective and save money. By embracing these practices, you can confidently navigate the complexities of taxes, ensuring you're well-prepared not just for the present year but for future financial success.

Chapter 9 - The Future of Taxes

As we navigate through an ever-evolving financial landscape, staying ahead of changes in tax laws becomes crucial. This chapter explores the future of taxes, focusing on potential changes in tax legislation, the emerging realm of digital currencies, and how to stay well-informed of new tax credits or deductions that could benefit you.

Question 23: How Might Tax Laws Change in the Future, and How Can I Stay Informed?

Tax laws are as dynamic as the economy; they adapt to reflect shifts in government policies, economic priorities, and societal needs. Changes can range from adjustments in tax rates to the introduction of new deductions and credits, impacting how much you owe or save each year.

Staying informed requires a proactive approach:

- **Follow Reputable Sources:** IRS websites, reputable financial news outlets, and tax-related blogs often provide timely updates on tax law changes.
- **Use IRS Resources:** The IRS offers a range of newsletters and social media updates tailored to different taxpayers, including

individuals, businesses, and tax professionals.
- **Consult Tax Professionals:** A trusted tax advisor can offer personalized insights into how changes affect your specific situation and suggest strategies to minimize your tax liability.

Question 24: What Are Digital Currencies, and How Are They Taxed?

Digital currencies, such as Bitcoin and Ethereum, have surged in popularity and acceptance, bringing them under the purview of tax authorities. In the eyes of the IRS, cryptocurrencies are treated as property, not currency. This means:

- **Capital Gains and Losses:** Buying and selling digital currencies can result in capital gains or losses, similar to trading stocks. You must report these transactions on your tax return.
- **Mining and Payment:** If you mine cryptocurrency or receive it as payment for goods or services, it's considered taxable income at its fair market value at the time of receipt.

Understanding the taxation of digital currencies is essential for anyone investing in or using them, emphasizing the need to keep detailed records of these transactions.

Question 25: Are There New Tax Credits or Deductions I Should Be Aware Of?

Tax credits and deductions evolve, with new ones introduced and others phased out, often reflecting current economic policies and social priorities. For example, recent years have seen incentives for clean energy, electric vehicles, and education. To stay on top of these changes:

- **Annual Tax Guides:** Look for updated tax guides and summaries highlighting new and expiring tax provisions each year.
- **Professional Advice:** Regular check-ins with a tax professional can help identify new opportunities for tax savings based on the latest laws.
- **Educational Workshops and Webinars:** Many organizations and financial institutions offer free workshops and webinars on tax planning, including updates on new tax laws.

The future of taxes is a blend of complexity and opportunity. You can confidently navigate future changes by staying informed, embracing technology, and seeking professional guidance. Whether adapting to new rules on digital currencies or leveraging the latest tax credits, a proactive approach to tax planning will help secure your financial future.

Conclusion

As we wrap up this journey through the world of taxes, it's clear that while the topic may seem daunting at first, approaching it with confidence and curiosity can transform what often feels like a chore into an empowering aspect of personal finance management. Taxes are not just a yearly obligation but a vital component of a broader financial strategy that can significantly impact your financial well-being when understood and managed well.

The tax system's complexity can overwhelm anyone, but remember, knowledge is power. Each chapter in this guide has equipped you with the tools and understanding needed to navigate taxes more confidently. You have a foundation to build upon, whether it's grasping the basics, optimizing deductions and credits, or planning for future changes. Taxes are an integral part of your financial landscape, and with each filing season, you can improve, learn, and even save money.

Curiosity leads to discovery. Don't hesitate to dig deeper into topics that impact your tax situation. The tax code is vast, and its nuances often work in your favor if you know where to look. Asking questions, whether of yourself, the internet, or professionals is the key to unlocking these opportunities. There's no such thing as a silly question, especially regarding taxes, where the answers can often lead to tangible financial benefits.

While this guide aims to make tax concepts more accessible, there's no substitute for personalized advice from a tax professional. Their expertise can clarify complex situations, such as significant life changes, investments, or navigating business taxes. A professional can also help you plan strategically, ensuring you're compliant and making decisions that enhance your overall financial health. Remember, investing in professional advice can pay dividends through tax savings and peace of mind.

Understanding and managing your taxes is a crucial skill in personal finance. Taxes touch almost every aspect of financial planning, from budgeting and saving to investing and retirement planning. Integrating tax strategies into your personal finance management allows you to make more informed decisions, optimize your savings, and even uncover opportunities to grow your wealth. Taxes are not just about meeting a legal obligation but about making informed choices that align with your financial goals.

As you move forward, carry the confidence from understanding taxes' role in your finances. Let curiosity guide your quest for knowledge, and don't shy away from seeking expert advice to navigate the intricacies of the tax system. Taxes are a part of life, but they can be managed effectively with the right approach, contributing to your financial success and stability.

In conclusion, approach taxes not as a daunting task but as a vital component of your financial toolkit. With each tax season, you have the opportunity to reinforce your financial foundation, ensuring that you're not only compliant but also capitalizing on opportunities to enhance

CONCLUSION

your financial future.

If you've found this book beneficial, please leave a review on Amazon.

Glossary: Understanding Key Tax Terms

Navigating the world of taxes means encountering a variety of terms that can sometimes seem like a foreign language. To help you better understand the discussions throughout this guide, here's a glossary of key tax terms mentioned, explained in simple, easy-to-understand language:

Adjusted Gross Income (AGI): Your total income for the year after deducting certain expenses like student loan interest or contributions to a traditional IRA. AGI is used to determine your eligibility for various tax credits and deductions.

Audit: An examination by the IRS to verify that your income, deductions, and credits are accurate as reported on your tax return. Audits can be random or triggered by discrepancies in your filing.

Capital Gains: The profit earned from the sale of assets like stocks or real estate. Long-term capital gains (on assets held for more than a year) are taxed at lower rates than ordinary income.

Deductions: Expenses that can be subtracted from your AGI to reduce your taxable income. Deductions can be itemized (specifically listed expenses) or standard (a flat amount allowed by the IRS).

GLOSSARY: UNDERSTANDING KEY TAX TERMS

Dependent: Someone you financially support, such as a child or relative, who can qualify you for certain tax benefits like credits or deductions.

Exemptions: Amounts that could be subtracted from your AGI based on the number of dependents you have.

Filing Status: Your tax filing category is based on your marital status and family situation. It affects your tax rates, standard deduction amounts, and eligibility for credits and deductions. Common statuses include Single, Married Filing Jointly, and Head of Household.

Income Tax: The tax on your earnings from work, investments, and other sources. The United States uses a progressive income tax system, where the rate increases as your income does.

IRS (Internal Revenue Service): The federal agency responsible for administering tax laws and collecting taxes in the United States.

Itemized Deductions: Specific expenses you can subtract from your AGI instead of taking the standard deduction. Common itemized deductions include mortgage interest, state and local taxes (SALT), and charitable donations.

Refundable Tax Credit: A credit that can reduce your tax liability to below zero, resulting in a refund. Examples include the Earned Income Tax Credit (EITC) and American Opportunity Tax Credit (AOTC).

Standard Deduction: A flat dollar amount that reduces your taxable income. It varies by filing status and is adjusted annually for inflation. Choosing the standard deduction simplifies filing and is beneficial if it's more than your total itemized deductions.

Tax Bracket: Categories determining the rate at which your income will be taxed. The U.S. tax system is progressive, meaning people with higher incomes pay higher tax rates on their income exceeding certain thresholds.

Tax Credit: An amount that directly reduces the tax you owe, dollar for dollar. Credits are more valuable than deductions because they reduce your tax bill directly rather than just lowering your taxable income.

Taxable Income: The portion of your income that is subject to income tax after all deductions and exemptions have been applied to your AGI.

Understanding these terms can explain the tax filing process, making it easier for you to navigate your taxes confidently. Whether you're tackling your tax return or planning for the future, having a grasp of these basics is crucial.

Useful Tools and Links for Managing Taxes

Navigating taxes can be smoother with the right resources at your fingertips. Whether you're looking for reliable information, tools to help with tax preparation, or professional advice, a wealth of resources is available online and in your community. Here's a list of websites, apps, tools, and contact information for obtaining tax assistance and advice.

Websites for Tax Information and Filing

1. **IRS.gov:** The official website of the Internal Revenue Service (IRS) is the go-to resource for authoritative tax information, forms, and tools, including the Free File program for those eligible.
2. **TaxpayerAdvocate.IRS.gov**: The Taxpayer Advocate Service is an independent organization within the IRS that helps taxpayers resolve problems and advocates for changes in the IRS.
3. **TurboTax.Intuit.com**: TurboTax offers guided tax preparation services for complex tax situations and simple filings, with options for expert review.
4. **HRBlock.com**: H&R Block provides tax filing solutions online and in-person, with a range of services from free basic filing to professional assistance.

GET ANSWERS TO YOUR TAX QUESTIONS

5. **TaxFoundation.org**: The Tax Foundation offers insights and analysis on tax policies at the federal and state levels for those interested in policy and the broader implications of tax laws.

Apps and Tools for Tax Management

1. **Mint**: By Intuit, Mint is a personal finance app that tracks spending. This can be useful for managing deductions and preparing for tax time.
2. **QuickBooks Self-Employed:** This app is tailored for freelancers and small business owners. It helps them track expenses and mileage and estimate taxes throughout the year.
3. **IRS2Go:** The IRS's official app lets you check your refund status, make payments, and find free tax preparation assistance.

Contact Information for Tax Assistance

- **IRS Help Line for Individuals**: 1-800-829-1040 - For personal tax questions, available Monday through Friday, 7 a.m. to 7 p.m. local time.
- **Taxpayer Advocate Service (TAS)**: 1-877-777-4778 - If you're experiencing economic harm or need help resolving tax problems that haven't been resolved through normal channels.
- **VITA (Volunteer Income Tax Assistance) Program**: Provides free tax help to people who generally make $57,000 or less, persons with disabilities, and limited English-speaking taxpayers. Visit the IRS website or call 1-800-906-9887 to find a VITA site near you.
- **AARP Foundation Tax-Aide**: offers free tax preparation for low-to-moderate-income taxpayers, especially those 50 and older. Visit

USEFUL TOOLS AND LINKS FOR MANAGING TAXES

the AARP site or call 1-888-227-7669 to locate a nearby service.

Utilizing these resources can make managing your taxes significantly more manageable, providing the guidance and support you need to navigate tax season confidently. Whether you prefer to handle tax preparation on your own or seek the help of professionals, there's a tool or service out there to suit your needs. Always remember to verify the credentials of any tax professional or service to ensure you're receiving accurate and reliable advice.

Resources

Hardison, R. (2023, July 19). Everything you need to know when dealing with the IRS for the first time. Imscouting. https://www.imscouting.com/dealing-with-the-irs-for-the-first-time/

Jeenat. (2024, January 29). What are education tax credits? A complete guide: 2024 – UnIACCO. UniAcco. https://uniacco.com/blog/what-are-education-tax-credits

Shri, I. (n.d.). Can I claim deductions for home office expenses as a sole proprietor? - Shri Associate. Shri Associate. https://shriassociate.com/faq-items/can-i-claim-deductions-for-home-office-expenses-as-a-sole-proprietor/

Temp, M., & Temp, M. (2023, March 1). Top tax tips. TOSTRUD & TEMP, S.C. https://www.tntcpas.com/2023/03/01/top-tax-tips/

U.S. News & World Report. (2023, February 28). The fastest way to get your tax refund. WTOP News. https://wtop.com/news/2023/02/the-fastest-way-to-get-your-tax-refund/

Wagner, M. (2023, July 30). What is the difference between gross and net pay Everfi? - ProfessionalLearningblog.com. Professional Learning

RESOURCES

Blog. http://professionallearningblog.com/what-is-the-difference-between-gross-and-net-pay-everfi/

Zenithtaxpro, & Zenithtaxpro. (2024, April 27). Unveil the secrets of efficient tax filing! - Zenith Tax Pro. Zenith Tax Pro - Provides Tax & Accounting Services. https://www.zenithtaxpro.com/maximize-your-returns-unveil-the-secrets-of-efficient-tax-filing/

www.ingramcontent.com/pod-product-compliance
Lightning Source LLC
Chambersburg PA
CBHW050027230526
45470CB00003B/1164